# GOVER TEX

## Local, State, and National Governments

### Sutter Cane

Rosen
Classroom™

New York

Published in 2010 by The Rosen Publishing Group, Inc.
29 East 21st Street, New York, NY 10010

Book Design: Daniel Hosek

Photo Credits: Cover, interior borders and backgrounds, pp. 12, 15 (seal),16–17, 29 (Capitol Building)
Shutterstock.com; p. 5 © Paul J. Richards/AFP/Getty Images; p. 7 © Frederic Lewis/Getty Images; pp. 8, 13
(top) courtesy Library of Congress; p. 9 courtesy Tarlton Law Library; p. 10 © Geoatlas; p. 13 (bottom)
© Amanda Edwards/Getty Images; p. 14 courtesy Wikimedia Commons; pp. 19, 22–23, 25 (map)
iStockphoto.com; p. 20 © Walter Bibikow/The Image Bank/Getty Images; p. 21 © Getty Images; p. 27 ©
David J. Sams/Photodisc/Getty Images; p. 28 © Jeff T. Green/Getty Images; p. 29 (top) © NASA/Getty Images;
p. 29 (middle) © Justin Sullivan/Getty Images; p. 29 (bottom) © Bill Pugliano/Getty Images.

Library of Congress Cataloging-in-Publication Data

Cane, Sutter.
 Governing Texas : local, state, and national governments / Sutter Cane.
     p. cm. — (Spotlight on Texas)
 Includes bibliographical references and index.
 ISBN 978-1-61532-483-5 (library binding)
 ISBN 978-1-61532-481-1 (pbk)
 ISBN 978-1-61532-482-8 (6-pack)
 1. Texas—Politics and government—Juvenile literature. I. Title.
 JK4816.C36 2010
 320.4764—dc22
                              2009031324

Manufactured in the United States of America

CPSIA Compliance Information: Batch # WW10RC: For further information contact Rosen Publishing, New York, New York at 1-800-237-9932.

# CONTENTS

# A Federal Government

Texas's government and **constitution** are modeled on the U.S. government and Constitution. This system of government is called federalism. A federal government is one in which power is divided between a central government and smaller area governments. This system is meant to give citizens power over local issues.

The Texas state government includes hundreds of workers called politicians. They work to keep the government running smoothly. Some politicians make laws. Others, such as the governor, **enforce** laws and oversee the government's daily business. Texas state courts and judges **interpret** the laws and settle **legal** problems.

Below the state government are other levels, including county, city, and town governments. Texas also recognizes three Native American governments.

The citizens of Texas vote for most of the politicians they want to govern the state.

# EARLY GOVERNMENTS IN TEXAS

Native American governments were the first to rule the area today known as Texas. There were more than twelve major Native American groups in Texas before Europeans arrived. Many were divided into smaller groups sometimes called bands. Most groups had their own forms of government. Some groups shared land and ways of life. Other groups didn't always get along.

Beginning in the 1500s, Europeans arrived and upset Native American ways of life. Many Indians died while fighting Europeans or from new illnesses the Europeans brought. The Spanish began building missions in Texas in 1690. Missions were meant to bring settlers and Indians together under Spanish rule. However, settlers often fought with Native Americans. Many Native Americans were forced out of Texas. Some stayed and lived under Spanish rule.

This picture shows a Comanche leader speaking to the people of his band. The Comanche Indians had moved into northern and central Texas by the 1800s. For many years, the Comanche—known as fierce warriors—stopped the Spanish from moving onto their lands.

# Missions and Empresarios

The Mexican government used the missions and men they called empresarios (ehm-preh-SAHR-yohz) to populate Texas. The empresarios brought large groups of settlers to Texas, most of whom were from the United States. The settlers began communities and farms around the missions. The empresarios were like local government leaders. However, they received only land and no real power from the Mexican government.

As more Americans moved to Texas, the Mexican government grew worried that the United States would try to take the area from them. They stopped allowing settlers to move to Texas. They also made trade between Texas and the United States harder. This made settlers angry. **Anglos** in Texas wanted more say in how they were governed.

Samuel Houston

Texas won its freedom from Mexico in 1836 and became an independent country. It quickly set up a new government with Samuel Houston—a hero of the Texas **Revolution**—as the first president. The government was patterned after the U.S. government.

The Texas government changed several times over the next 30 years. Texas became a U.S. state in 1845, but left the country and fought against it during the **American Civil War**. Texas once again became a U.S. state in 1870.

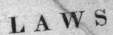

# LAWS

OF THE

# REPUBLIC OF TEXAS,

IN TWO VOLUMES.

PRINTED BY ORDER OF THE SECRETARY OF STATE.

Volume I.

HOUSTON:
PRINTED AT THE OFFICE OF THE TELEGRAPH.
1838.

When Texas became an independent country in 1836, the writers of its constitution copied some sections directly from the U.S. Constitution. Other sections were based on Mexican laws.

# TEXAS STATE GOVERNMENT TODAY

The Texas state government is made up of three equal but separate parts called branches. These include the executive branch (led by the governor), the legislative branch (lawmakers), and the judicial branch (courts). Each branch has its own powers. Each is kept from being too strong by the powers of the other two branches. In this way, the Texas state government—like the U.S. federal government—is ruled by a system of "checks and balances." Together, the three branches make sure the government runs smoothly and guards the rights of Texas citizens.

AUSTIN

The city of Austin has been the center of Texas government since 1839.

# The Texas State Constitution

Texas has had seven constitutions since 1827. The current constitution was written in 1876. The writers wanted to correct a problem of the earlier constitution, which many people thought gave the governor too much power. It's one of the longest state constitutions because of the large number of amendments it has. Amendments are changes made to a constitution to fix problems. For example, an amendment added in 1919 gave women in Texas the right to vote.

**first constitution**
Texas is part of a Mexican state called Coahuila (koh-ah-WEE-lah) and Texas.

1827

**second constitution**
Texas wins its independence from Mexico and becomes a country.

1836

**third constitution**
Texas becomes a U.S. state.

1845

**fourth constitution**
Texas joins the South during the American Civil War.

1861

**fifth constitution**
U.S. government tells Texas to write a new constitution.

1866

**sixth constitution**
Texas prepares to reenter the Union (1870).

1869

**seventh constitution**
Texas adopts the constitution still in use today.

1876

# THE EXECUTIVE BRANCH

The Texas executive branch enforces laws. The governor is the top official in this branch. Texans worried that the governor was too powerful under the 1869 constitution. So the 1876 constitution limited the powers of the governor by dividing executive duties among many elected officials. This is why the office of the governor is often called a "weak" position.

The governor is elected by the people. He or she serves a 4-year term and may be reelected. The governor is part of a team of officials who lead the state. The governor appoints the secretary of state, but voters elect all other team officials. The governor appoints officials to special boards with the consent of the state senate.

## ● POWERS OF THE TEXAS GOVERNOR

- sign bills into state law or veto (say no to) them
- call special meetings of the Texas legislature
- set government plans and rules
- help decide how state funds are used
- appoint officials to state boards
- in charge of the Texas military

Miriam Ferguson

Ann Richards

Miriam Ferguson became Texas's first female governor in 1925. Ann Richards became the second in 1991.

The lieutenant governor is the second-highest elected official in the Texas state government. This official is often thought to be the most powerful Texas politician. The lieutenant governor is the president of the state senate. The lieutenant governor directs the lawmaking system. He or she also forms special boards to discuss important topics. If the governor can't fulfill his or her duties, the lieutenant governor takes over.

The executive branch also includes many important agencies. An agency is a government body that oversees important businesses and services. For example, the Railroad Commission controls railroads, oil, gas, mining, and trucking in Texas. Other state agencies control farming, banking, education, family services, parks, and even films and music.

# The Plural Executive

In the national government, the president appoints many of the officials in the executive branch. In Texas, citizens elect nearly all of the members of the executive branch. All executive officials share executive power. This is called a plural executive.

- Governor—head of the executive branch
- Lieutenant Governor—president of the senate
- Attorney General—chief legal officer of the state
- Comptroller of Public Accounts—main tax officer of the state
- Commissioner of Agriculture—oversees state farming
- Commissioner of the General Land Office—oversees public lands
- Secretary of State—chief officer of state election laws (only appointed position)

Shown here is the front of the Texas Governor's Mansion in Austin. It was built in 1856. Fire destroyed part of the building in 2008. It has since been fixed.

# The Legislative Branch

The Texas legislature makes state laws. Members of the legislative branch **represent** the citizens of Texas in the lawmaking system. The Texas legislature is made up of two parts or houses. They are called the senate and the house of representatives.

There are thirty-one senators in the Texas senate. Each senator represents a **district** with about 672,000 people. The lieutenant governor is the leader of the senate. The house has 150 representatives. Each member of the house represents a district with about 140,000 people. The speaker of the house is elected to be the leader by the other house members.

The lieutenant governor and speaker of the house appoint members of the legislature to committees. Committees are smaller groups that solve problems, study issues, and write laws for the rest of the legislature to vote on.

The Texas state capitol building in Austin, shown here, was completed in 1888. It is made of a stone called red granite. In 1986, it became a National Historic Landmark.

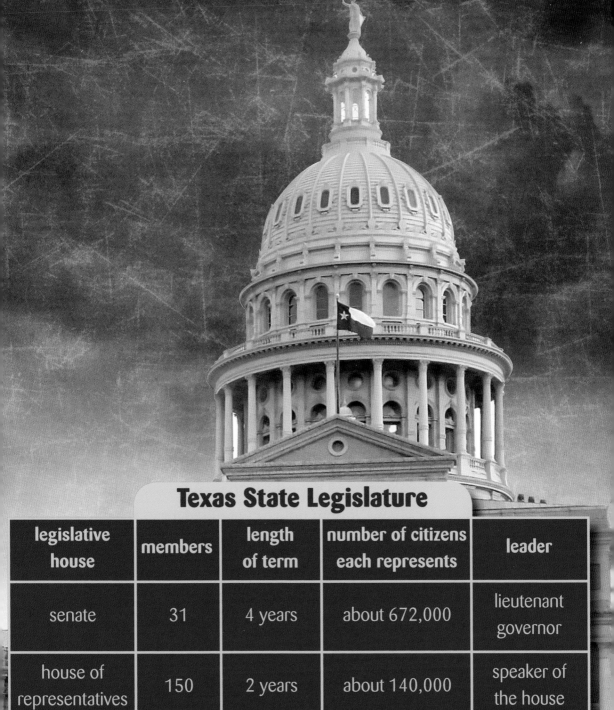

## Texas State Legislature

| legislative house | members | length of term | number of citizens each represents | leader |
|---|---|---|---|---|
| senate | 31 | 4 years | about 672,000 | lieutenant governor |
| house of representatives | 150 | 2 years | about 140,000 | speaker of the house |

The legislature begins a new regular **session** once every 2 years. The first meeting occurs on the second Tuesday of odd-numbered years. Regular sessions last no longer than 140 days. Members of the legislature have other jobs when they're not in session. The governor can call a special session if needed. Special sessions last no longer than 30 days.

In addition to making laws, the Texas legislature has other important powers. For example, it decides how to use state funds.

# How Laws Are Made

The lawmaking systems of the U.S. Congress and the Texas legislature are very much alike. First, an idea called a bill is read before the house or senate. Then a special committee talks about it. If the committee thinks the bill is a good idea, the entire house or senate votes on it. If it passes the vote, it's sent to the other house for a vote. If both houses vote in favor of the bill, it goes to the governor.

The governor may sign the bill into law. The governor may also veto the bill, which means he or she decides not to sign it. However, if two-thirds of the members of both houses vote in favor of the bill a second time, it becomes a law.

This is the Texas state Senate Chamber, which is where Texas senators meet.

# THE JUDICIAL BRANCH

The judicial branch of Texas government is made up of many courts and judges. The judicial branch interprets state laws. It says how laws should be enforced. It also holds **trials**. Texas's judicial branch includes local, county, and state courts.

The Texas judicial system hears two types of cases. Civil cases decide arguments between citizens, businesses, and government officials. They often concern things like money, property, and family legal matters. Criminal cases are held to decide if someone broke the law. If a court finds that the person broke the law, the court also decides how to **punish** them.

Presidio County Courthouse in Marfa, Texas

Texas district judge Belinda Hill speaks in front of a Texas court in 2006.

There are two kinds of courts in Texas. Trial courts hear cases and come to a decision. When a person on trial doesn't agree with the decision, they may "file an appeal." The case is heard in a court of appeals to decide if the first trial followed the state law.

Shown here is the DeWitt County courtroom in Cuero, Texas.

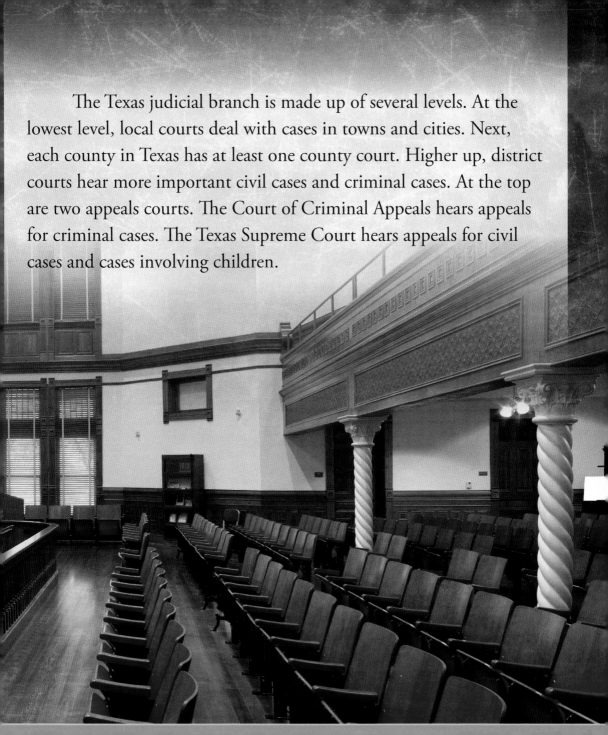

The Texas judicial branch is made up of several levels. At the lowest level, local courts deal with cases in towns and cities. Next, each county in Texas has at least one county court. Higher up, district courts hear more important civil cases and criminal cases. At the top are two appeals courts. The Court of Criminal Appeals hears appeals for criminal cases. The Texas Supreme Court hears appeals for civil cases and cases involving children.

# LOCAL GOVERNMENTS IN TEXAS

Just like state and national governments, local Texas governments have three branches and are ruled by a system of checks and balances. Local governments include town, city, and county governments.

There are 254 counties in Texas, each with its own government. County governments help the state and federal governments do their jobs. County officials include sheriffs, county judges, clerks, and tax officials. Each county is divided into four districts. Each district is represented by an official called a commissioner. Commissioners help make county laws and oversee county business. County governments build and maintain county roads, bridges, hospitals, airports, and other county property.

Texas counties are organized into twenty-four districts (colored regions) led by governments called councils of government. A council of government addresses issues that are important to all the counties in a district. These may include water supplies, national security, and economic growth.

# Tribal Governments in Texas

Texas has three Native American governments that are recognized by the federal government. These groups live on tribally owned land called reservations. They are the Kickapoo in southern Texas, the Alabama-Coushatta in eastern Texas, and the Ysleta del Sur Pueblo in western Texas. The federal government recognizes them as **sovereign** nations free from outside control. This means that the national and state governments recognize their right to govern their people within the borders of their reservations.

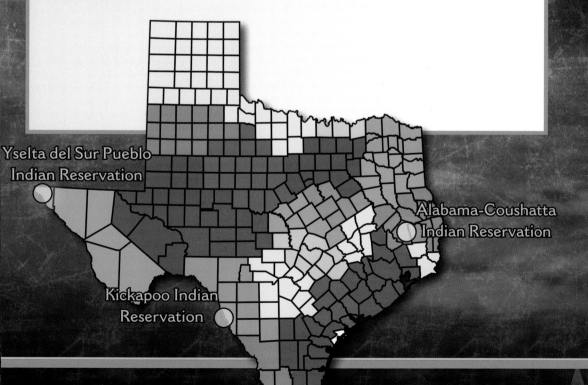

Yselta del Sur Pueblo Indian Reservation

Alabama-Coushatta Indian Reservation

Kickapoo Indian Reservation

Local governments in Texas provide citizens with services the state government doesn't provide. These services include trash removal, education, police departments, and fire departments. Local governments collect taxes to help pay for services.

Many Texas towns have a strong executive leader called a mayor. Most cities have a mayor-council or council-manager government. Mayor-council governments have a weak mayor and are led by a powerful group of elected officials called a council. In a council-manager government, the council appoints a manager to oversee the operation of the local government.

In addition to towns, cities, and counties, Texas also has special districts that require government bodies. Special districts include school systems, water supplies, public hospitals, and road systems.

Firefighters and police officers face danger in order to keep the communities they serve safe.

# TEXANS IN OUR NATIONAL GOVERNMENT

Texas citizens elect politicians to represent them in the U.S. government, just as voters in other states do. All states have two senators in the U.S. Senate. The number of politicians each state has in the U.S. House of Representatives is based on the state's population. As one of the larger states, Texas has thirty-two representatives in the House.

Texans have also served in the judicial and executive branches

Sandra Day O'Connor

of national government. Sandra Day O'Connor—who was born in El Paso, Texas—was the first woman to serve on the U.S. Supreme Court. Three U.S. presidents were first Texas politicians: Lyndon Johnson, George H. W. Bush, and George W. Bush. Texas politicians have truly helped shape our nation.

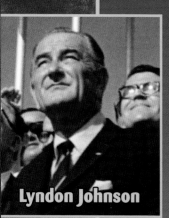

Lyndon Johnson

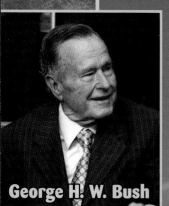

George H. W. Bush

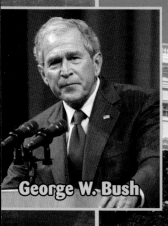

George W. Bush

U.S. Congress meets in the U.S. Capitol Building in Washington, D.C., shown here.

# READER RESPONSE PROJECTS

- Use your town or city newspaper to find a story about an issue facing local, state, or national government. How do you feel about the issue? Write a letter to the editor explaining your opinion.

- Which branch of Texas government would you like to learn more about? Create a table like the one shown here:

| what I know | what I want to know | what I learned |
| --- | --- | --- |
|  |  |  |

In the first column, write three things you learned about one branch of Texas government. In the middle column, write three things you would still like to know about that topic. Use the library and the Internet to answer the questions and write them in the last column.

- Write a letter to a state senator or representative telling him or her about an idea you have for a law. Clearly explain what you think the law should say and why you think there's a need for it.

# GLOSSARY

**American Civil War** (uh-MEHR-uh-kuhn SIH-vuhl WOHR) A war between the Northern and Southern states fought from 1861 to 1865.

**Anglo** (AYN-gloh) Someone who speaks English and whose family came from a part of Europe other than Spain.

**constitution** (kahn-stuh-TOO-shun) The basic rules by which a country or state is governed.

**district** (DIHS-trihkt) A smaller area of a state or county that has its own government.

**enforce** (ehn-FOHRS) To carry out.

**interpret** (ihn-TUHR-pruht) To explain the meaning of something.

**legal** (LEE-guhl) Having to do with laws.

**punish** (PUH-nish) To cause someone pain or loss for a crime.

**represent** (reh-prih-ZEHNT) To speak for a person or group of people.

**revolution** (reh-vuh-LOO-shun) An organized attempt to overthrow the government in power.

**session** (SEH-shun) A meeting of an official body.

**sovereign** (SAH-vuh-ruhn) Free from outside control.

**trial** (TRYL) A case decided in court.

# INDEX

## A
amendment(s), 11
attorney general, 15

## B
Bush, George H. W., 28
Bush, George W., 28

## C
checks and balances, 10, 24
civil cases, 20, 23
commissioner of agriculture, 15
commissioner of the General Land Office, 15
comptroller of public accounts, 15
constitution(s), 4, 11, 12
court(s), 4, 10, 20, 22, 23
Court of Criminal Appeals, 23
criminal cases, 20, 23

## E
executive branch, 10, 12, 14, 15, 28

## G
governor, 4, 10, 11, 12, 14, 15, 18

## H
house of representatives, 16, 17, 18
Houston, Samuel, 8

## J
Johnson, Lyndon, 28
judges, 4, 20, 24
judicial branch, 10, 20, 23, 28

## L
law(s), 4, 12, 15, 16, 18, 20, 22, 24, 30
legislative branch, 10, 16
legislature, 12, 16, 17, 18
lieutenant governor, 14, 15, 16, 17
local government(s), 24, 26, 30

## N
Native American governments, 4, 6, 25

## O
O'Connor, Sandra Day, 28

## P
plural executive, 15

## S
secretary of state, 12, 15
senate, 12, 14, 15, 16, 17, 18
speaker of the house, 16, 17
special districts, 26
state government, 4, 10, 14, 24, 25, 26, 30

## T
Texas Supreme Court, 23
trial courts, 22

## U
U.S. Constitution, 4
U.S. House of Representatives, 28
U.S. Senate, 28
U.S. Supreme Court, 28

## V
veto, 12, 18

Due to the changing nature of Internet links, the Rosen Publishing Group, Inc., has developed an online list of Web sites related to the subject of this book. This site is updated regularly. Please use this link to access the list: **http://www.rcbmlinks.com/sot/govtex/**